ALL ABOUT ARACHNIDS
JUMPING SPIDERS

by Becca Becker

Ideas for Parents and Teachers

Pogo Books let children practice reading informational text while introducing them to nonfiction features such as headings, labels, sidebars, maps, and diagrams, as well as a table of contents, glossary, and index.

Carefully leveled text with a strong photo match offers early fluent readers the support they need to succeed.

Before Reading

- "Walk" through the book and point out the various nonfiction features. Ask the student what purpose each feature serves.
- Look at the glossary together. Read and discuss the words.

Read the Book

- Have the child read the book independently.
- Invite them to list questions that arise from reading.

After Reading

- Discuss the child's questions. Talk about how they might find answers to those questions.
- Prompt the child to think more. Ask: What did you know about jumping spiders before reading this book? What more would you like to learn about them?

Pogo Books are published by Jump!
5357 Penn Avenue South
Minneapolis, MN 55419
www.jumplibrary.com

Copyright © 2025 Jump! International copyright reserved in all countries. No part of this book may be reproduced in any form without written permission from the publisher.

Library of Congress Cataloging-in-Publication Data

Names: Becker, Becca, author.
Title: Jumping spiders / by Becca Becker.
Description: Minneapolis, MN: Jump!, Inc., [2025]
Series: All about arachnids | Includes index.
Audience: Ages 7-10
Identifiers: LCCN 2024034846 (print)
LCCN 2024034847 (ebook)
ISBN 9798892136181 (hardcover)
ISBN 9798892136198 (paperback)
ISBN 9798892136204 (ebook)
Subjects: LCSH: Jumping spiders—Juvenile literature.
Jumping spiders—Life cycles—Juvenile literature.
Classification: LCC QL458.42.S24 B43 2025 (print)
LCC QL458.42.S24 (ebook)
DDC 595.4/4—dc23/eng/20240830
LC record available at https://lccn.loc.gov/2024034846
LC ebook record available at https://lccn.loc.gov/2024034847

Editor: Katie Chanez
Designer: Emma Almgren-Bersie

Photo Credits: nelaco/iStock, cover; Chase D'animulls/Shutterstock, 1; Pichit Sansupa/Shutterstock, 3, 23; Fresnelwiki/Wikimedia, 4; Chris Robbins/Alamy, 5; memcockers/iStock, 6-7; Scott Linstead/Science Source, 8-9; John Burnham/Alamy, 10-11; David Havel/Shutterstock, 12; Danny Radius/Shutterstock, 13; crbellette/iStock, 14-15tl; Silapavet Konthikamee/Shutterstock, 14-15tr; Clarence Holmes Wildlife/Alamy, 14-15bl; Sarefo/Wikimedia, 14-15br; Bildagentur Zoonar GmbH/Shutterstock, 16-17; Somyot Mali-ngam/Shutterstock, 18, 19; Niney Azman/Shutterstock, 20-21.

Printed in the United States of America at Corporate Graphics in North Mankato, Minnesota.

TABLE OF CONTENTS

CHAPTER 1
Small Jumpers..4

CHAPTER 2
All Around the World....................................12

CHAPTER 3
Life Cycle..18

ACTIVITIES & TOOLS
Try This!...22
Glossary...23
Index..24
To Learn More..24

CHAPTER 1
SMALL JUMPERS

A small spider uses its eight legs to crawl up a plant. It sees an **insect**. It jumps for it. What is this **arachnid**? It is a jumping spider!

Before every jump, a jumping spider lets out a thread of silk. It sticks to where the spider stands. Then the spider jumps. If it misses its target, the silk catches it. It keeps the spider from falling to the ground. The spider climbs up the silk. It jumps again!

silk

CHAPTER 1   5

These spiders jump in a special way. They move fluids in their body to do it. Some jump up to 30 times their body length!

CHAPTER 1

TAKE A LOOK!

How do jumping spiders jump? Take a look!

① The spider lets out a silk thread. It attaches to where it stands.

② The spider moves fluids in its body. It pushes fluids to its feet.

③ The fluid makes the spider's legs longer.

④ The spider jumps!

CHAPTER 1

Jumping spiders jump to get around. They jump to escape **predators**. They jump to catch **prey**, too. They eat insects like flies and grasshoppers.

CHAPTER 1

CHAPTER 1

Some jumping spiders eat other spiders! How? A jumping spider finds another spider's web. It shakes the web. The other spider thinks an insect is stuck. It crawls over. The jumping spider attacks!

DID YOU KNOW?

After catching prey, the jumping spider bites it. It sucks up the prey's insides. Yum!

CHAPTER 1

CHAPTER 2
ALL AROUND THE WORLD

Jumping spiders live everywhere but Antarctica. They are found in many **habitats**. Some live in wet rain forests. Others are in dry deserts. The spiders live on cold mountains, too.

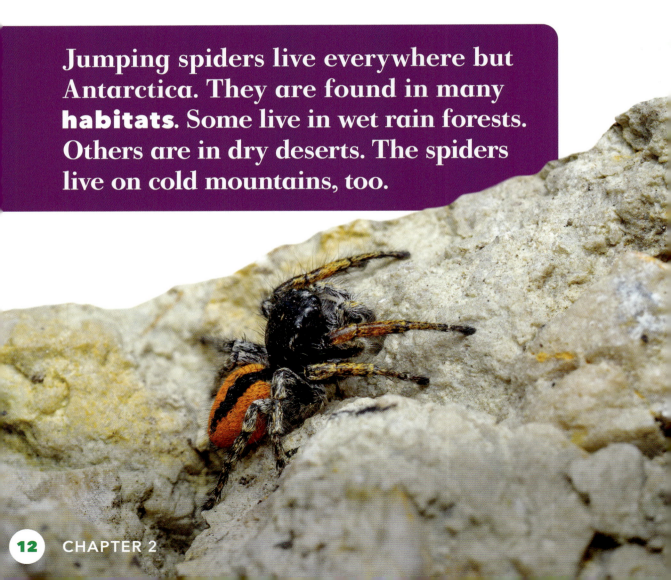

Jumping spiders make small silk shelters. Where? They do this under bark, leaves, or stones. They stay in their shelters at night. They come out to hunt during the day.

CHAPTER 2   13

Some jumping spiders are colorful. The peacock jumping spider has red, green, and yellow. It is named after a peacock's colorful feathers. The regal jumping spider has colorful **chelicerae**.

Others have dull colors. The tan jumping spider can be tan, brown, gray, or black. It blends in. The southeast Asian jumping spider looks like an ant! Why? Some predators won't eat ants.

DID YOU KNOW?

There are more than 5,000 jumping spider **species**. All are less than one inch (2.5 centimeters) long.

peacock jumping spider

regal jumping spider

tan jumping spider

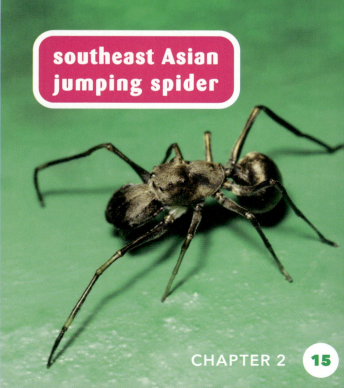
southeast Asian jumping spider

CHAPTER 2

Jumping spiders have eight eyes. Four face forward. The others are on the side of the head. This helps them see all around. Jumping spiders have the best eyesight of all spiders.

TAKE A LOOK!

What are the parts of a jumping spider? Take a look!

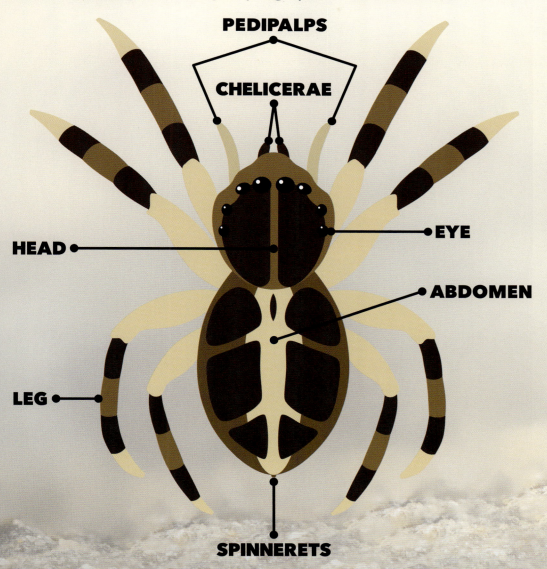

CHAPTER 2   17

CHAPTER 3
LIFE CYCLE

Adult jumping spiders **mate**. Then the female lays eggs. She wraps them in silk to make an egg sac. She puts the egg sac under a leaf or other object. Why? It is hidden from predators. It is also safe from bad weather.

egg sac

The **spiderlings** hatch. They stay with mom until they are old enough to live on their own.

spiderlings

CHAPTER 3 19

As a spider grows, it **molts**. It may use its silk to make a saclike space. It crawls in it to molt. When the spider is ready to move again, it jumps away!

DID YOU KNOW?

People have trained jumping spiders. One jumped on command!

ACTIVITIES & TOOLS

TRY THIS!

JUMP ACROSS

Jumping spiders jump from place to place. How many jumps does it take to cross a room? Find out with this fun activity!

What You Need:
- an open room
- a few friends
- pencil and paper

❶ Find an open room or clear enough space in a room. Ask an adult for help if needed.

❷ Stand at one end of the room. Jump to the other end! Count each jump you take.

❸ How many jumps did it take to cross the room? Write the number down.

❹ Have your friends jump across the room, too. How many jumps did it take them? How do your jumps compare?

GLOSSARY

arachnid: A creature with a body divided into two parts, such as a spider or a scorpion.

chelicerae: Jaws arachnids have that hold prey.

habitats: Places where animals or plants are usually found.

insect: A small animal with three pairs of legs, one or two pairs of wings, and three main body parts.

mate: To come together to produce babies.

molts: Sheds an outer layer.

predators: Animals that hunt other animals for food.

prey: Animals hunted by other animals for food.

species: One of the groups into which similar animals and plants are divided.

spiderlings: Baby spiders.

ACTIVITIES & TOOLS 23

INDEX

bites 11
catches 5, 8, 11
chelicerae 14, 17
egg sac 18
eyesight 16
habitats 12
hunt 13
insect 4, 8, 11
jumps 4, 5, 6, 7, 8, 20
mate 18
molts 20

peacock jumping spider 14
predators 8, 14, 18
prey 8, 11
regal jumping spider 14
shelters 13
silk 5, 7, 13, 18, 20
southeast Asian jumping spider 14
species 14
spiderlings 19
tan jumping spider 14
web 11

TO LEARN MORE

Finding more information is as easy as 1, 2, 3.

1. Go to www.factsurfer.com
2. Enter "jumpingspiders" into the search box.
3. Choose your book to see a list of websites.

24 ACTIVITIES & TOOLS